Little Blue Dot

3

Bridget Kelly

Activity Book

OXFORD
UNIVERSITY PRESS

MODULE	UNIT	VOCABULARY	STRUCTURES	PHONICS	VALUES & FUNCTIONAL LANGUAGE	EXPLORE	PROJECT
Our communities p.4 Concept: *community* numbers 21–30	**Unit 1 People we know p.6** **Generalization:** *We belong to more than one community.*	watch TV, play board games, ride bikes, skateboard, dress up, dance cook, nurse, cleaner, principal, teacher, bus driver doctor, police officer, firefighter, dentist	We (watch TV). There's a fire! She's/He's a (teacher).	/oʊ/ with **o_e** (hose) and **ow** (bow)	**Ask for help** I/We need help!	Community helpers	Make a poster about one of your communities.
	Unit 2 Places we go p.16 **Generalization:** *Communities share the same places.*	hospital, beach, sports center, playground, library, community garden plastic, glass, metal, paper, bin, recycle dig soil, plant seeds, pull up weeds, pick fruit/vegetables	Where are you/they? We're/They're at the (hospital). It needs water. Where do we put (metal)? In the (blue) bin. We (plant seeds).	/i/ with **ea** (peach) and **ee** (seed)	**Look after plants** Let's water the plants.	Growing plants	Plant a seed and look after it as it grows.
	Unit 3 Party time! p.26 **Generalization:** *Communities celebrate together.*	costume, present, cake, decorations, cards, candles invitation, birthday, months of the year festival, music, lantern, fireworks	There's a (costume). There are (decorations). This festival is in (July).	/eɪ/ with **a_e** (lake) and **ai** (snail)	**Make things for your friends** This is for you.	Festivals	Make a paper lantern.
	Now I know Units 1–3 p.36						
	Story time: Zucchinis galore! **p.38**						
Let's create! p.40 Concept: *creativity* numbers 40, 50, 60, 70, puppet show, mask, stage	**Unit 4 Things we make p.42** **Generalization:** *We use different materials to create things.*	tape, scissors, paint, paintbrush, camera, clay tennis, racket drawing, painting, sticking, printing, making models, taking photos short line, long line, straight line, curved line	Do you have the (tape)? Yes, I do. / No, I don't. We don't have a ball. I like (paint)ing. There are (two) (long) lines.	/u/ with **oo** (boot) and **ue** (glue)	**Be resourceful** Let's think. We can use this. Good idea!	Different lines in artwork	Make a class quilt.
	Unit 5 Stories p.52 **Generalization:** *Stories help us to explore feelings and develop creativity.*	laugh, frown, yawn, whisper, shout, make a face bear, king, superhero, child, wolf, scarecrow light, dark, shadow, flashlight	(Shout), then (yawn). Please don't shout. Is she/he a (bear)? Yes, she/he is. / No, she/he isn't.	/aɪ/ with **igh** (light) and **i_e** (hide)	**Respect others** Please don't shout. Sorry.	Shadows and puppets	Create a puppet and act out a story.

MODULE	UNIT	VOCABULARY	STRUCTURES	PHONICS	VALUES & FUNCTIONAL LANGUAGE	EXPLORE	PROJECT
Let's create! p.40 Concept: *creativity* numbers 40, 50, 60, 70, puppet show, mask, stage	**Unit 6 Let's make music! p.62** **Generalization:** *There are lots of types of music and they can make us feel different emotions.*	(playing the) guitar, piano, trumpet, recorder, (banging the) drum, (shaking the) tambourine fast, slow, high, low, loud, quiet scared, calm, excited, cheerful	She's/He's (playing the guitar). This is fun! This music is (fast). This music makes me feel (cheerful).	/ar/ with **ar** (harp, shark)	**Cheer your friends up** I'm sad. Let's cheer you up.	Music and feelings	Make a homemade drum.
	Now I know Units 4–6 p.72						
	Story time: What is music? p.74						
On the move p.76 Concept: *movement* land, air, water, numbers 80, 90, 100	**Unit 7 Let's go! p.78** **Generalization:** *We use different transportation in different situations.*	bus, boat, car, plane, train, walk helmet, hot air balloon truck, fire truck, motorcycle, taxi, tractor, helicopter rocket, astronaut, spacesuit, space	Let's go by (bus). Let's (walk). She/He (drives) a (truck). She/He (flies) a (helicopter).	/ər/ with **er** (scooter, soccer)	**Travel safely** We need to wear our helmets.	Space travel	Make a paper plane.
	Unit 8 Animal action p.88 **Generalization:** *Animals can move in different ways.*	rabbit, snake, tiger, monkey, dolphin, lizard crawl, slither, leap, hop, swing, climb spider, kangaroo, race webbed feet, strong legs, long tail, smooth body	Do (rabbits) have (legs)? Yes, they do. / No, they don't. Spiders (crawl).	/ɔ/ with **aw** (paw, claw)	**Be active to feel good** I (don't) feel great.	Animal adaptations	Make a paper chain snake.
	Unit 9 Adventures p.98 **Generalization:** *We move differently in different places.*	forest, ocean, desert, city, farm, mountains shelter skiing, sailing, surfing, skating, zip-lining, riding a horse spring, summer, fall, winter	I'd like to go to the (forest). Is she/he (skiing)? Yes, she/he is. / No, she/he isn't.	/aʊ/ with **ow** (town) and **ou** (campground)	**Accept challenges** Would you like to build a shelter? Yes, I would.	Seasons	Make a landscape.
	Now I know Units 7–9 p.118						
	Story time: Ollie's ocean adventure p.110						

Our communities

1 Look and match.

2 🔊 001 Listen, read, and circle **Yes** or **No**.

1 There's a party.   (Yes)   No

2 There's a baby.   Yes   No

3 It's sunny.   Yes   No

4 There's a pineapple.   Yes   No

5 There's a big tree.   Yes   No

1 🔊002 Listen and check ✓.

A 

B 

C 

2 Color and count. Write and say.

1 People we know

1 Look and circle.

2 Choose a person in your family or a friend. Draw something you do together.

grandma

friend

mom

friends

grandpa

mom

sister

dad

brother

mom

grandma

sister

1 Read and number.

| **1** watch TV | **2** dress up | **3** play board games |
| **4** dance | **5** ride bikes | **6** skateboard |

2 Look, complete, and say.

We s__a_e o r together.

1 🔊 003 Listen and check ✓ the words with the /oʊ/ sound.

2 🔊 004 Listen and color.

① 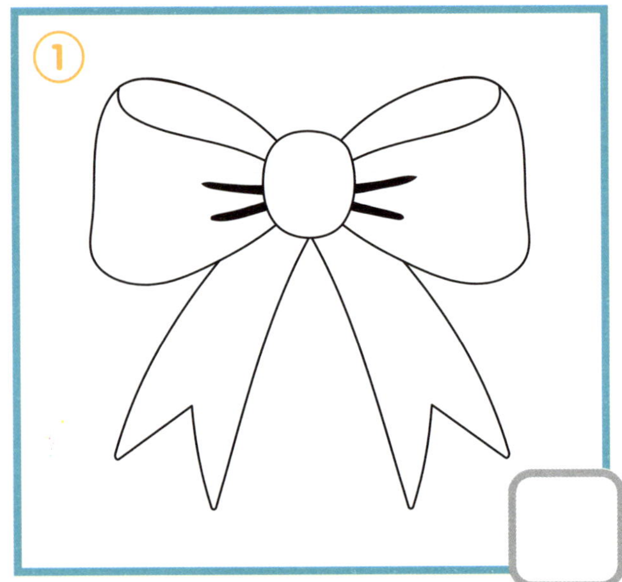

② 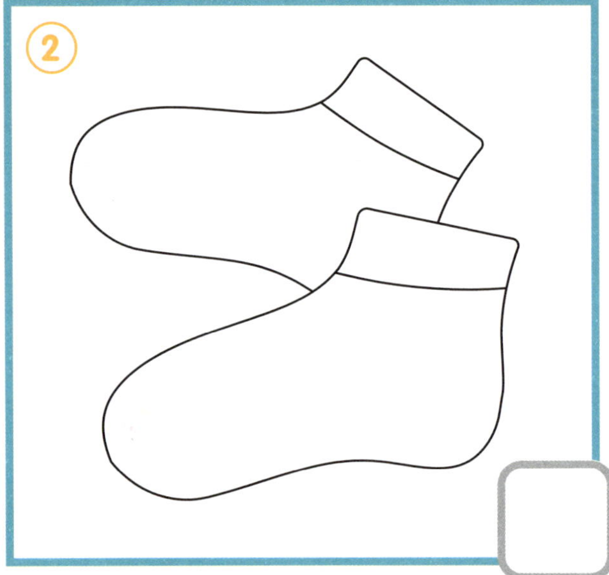

③ 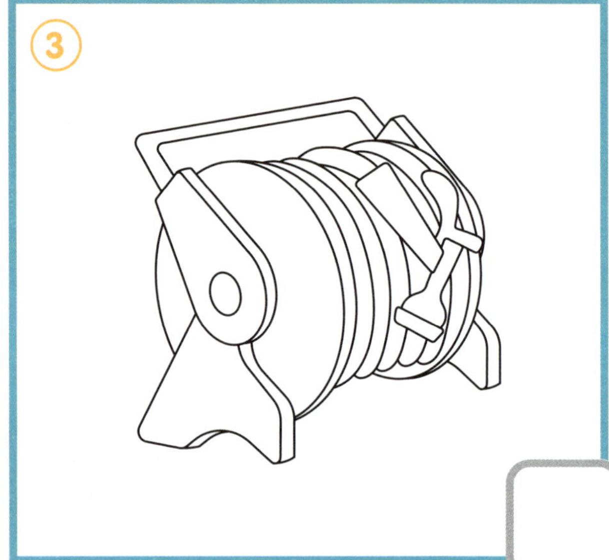

④ 

⑤ 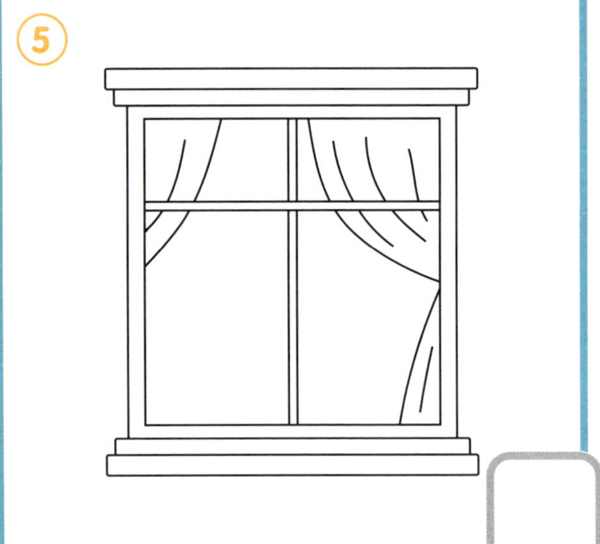

⑥ 

Lesson 3 Phonics   **Language focus:** /oʊ/ sound with *o_e (hose)* and *ow (bow)*

1 Read and number. Tell the story.

2 Who has a blue skateboard? Circle.

1 Who needs help? Look and circle.　　**2** Trace. Match and say.

Lesson 5 Value　　**Value:** ask for help　　**Language focus:** *I/We need help!*

1 Look and complete. **2** 🔊 005 Listen and check ✓ the correct picture.

cleaner ~~nurse~~ cook teacher driver principal

①

A

He's a
n **u** r **s** e.

B

He's a
c __ __ k.

②

A

She's a
t __ ach __ r.

B

She's a
bus __ r __ ver.

③

A

She's a
pri __ c __ pal.

B

She's a
__ lean __ __ .

3 Look and write the sentence.

principal. a He's

________ ________

____

1 Look and circle. **2** Think and color the clothes you see in your community.

police officer

firefighter

cleaner

doctor

firefighter

teacher

doctor

dentist

Lesson 7 Explore: community helpers   **Language focus:** *He's/She's a doctor / police officer / firefighter / dentist.*

1 🔊006 Listen and tick ✔ the box.

1
A B

2
A B

3
A B

4
A B

1 🔊 007 Listen and number.

(A)

(B)

(C)

(D)

2 Look at the posters in your classroom. How many are there for each community?

Lesson 9 Project **Language focus:** *This is (my mom). There's a (firefighter).*

1 Read and match.

1 She's a bus driver.

2 We ride bikes.

3 She's a dentist.

4 He's a cleaner.

5 We dress up.

6 We watch TV.

A   B   C   D   E   F

2 Read and draw.

He's a firefighter.

2 Places we go

1 🔊008 Listen and circle the correct picture.

2 Trace and say.

A

B

street   house

A

B

school   apartment

A

B

supermarket   park

3 Draw a place you often go to.
Who do you see there? Say.

1 Look and write. **2** 🔊 009 Listen and match.

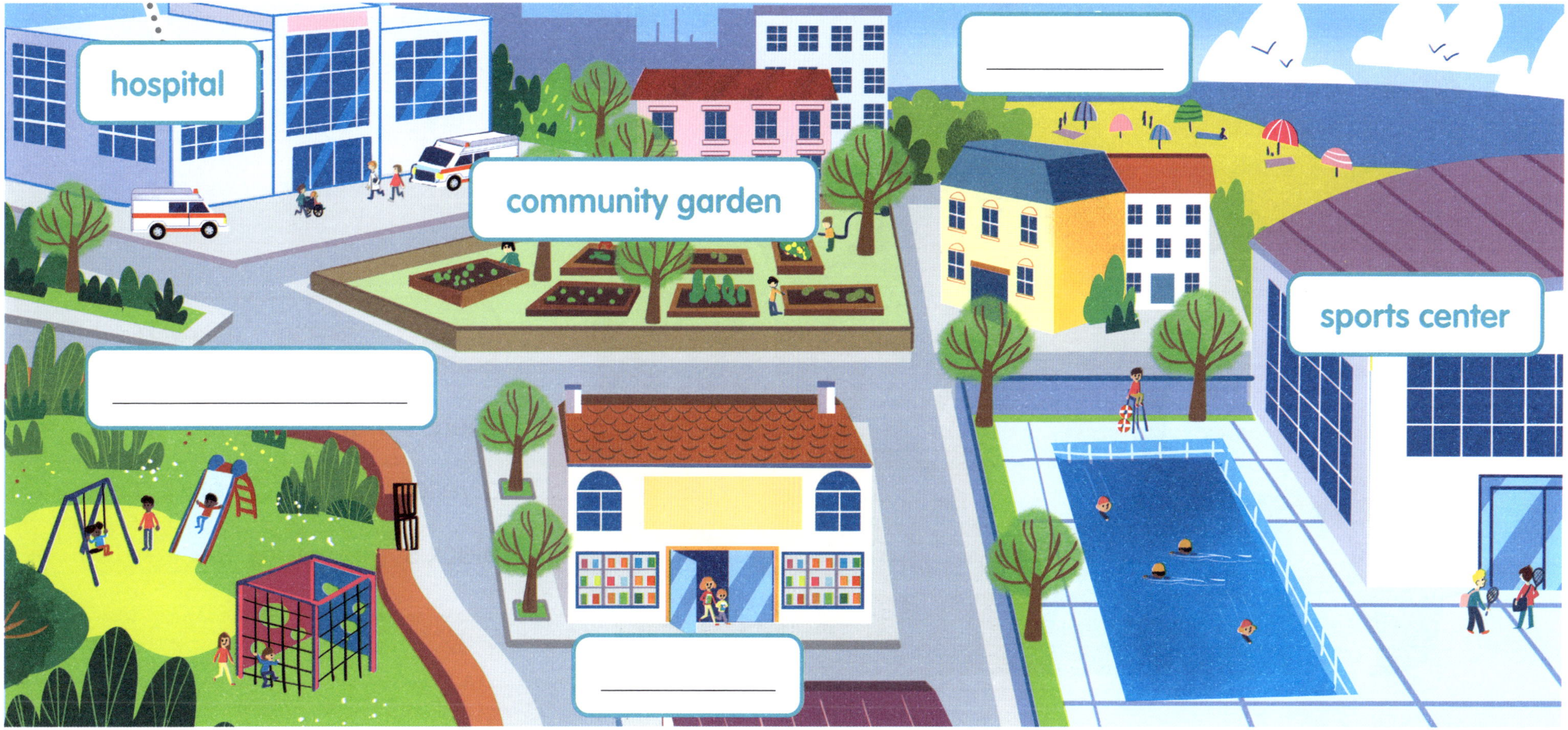

1 🔊010 Listen, read, and complete.

bee   peach

There's a b __ __ on the p __ __ch.

2 🔊011 Listen and color. Complete.

leaf   seed   green

There's a gr __ __n leaf and a yellow l __ __f. There's a black s __ __d.

1 🔊 012 Read and circle. Listen and check. **2** What does the tree need? Circle.  

1 Circle the plants that need help. **2** Check ✓ the ways to help. **3** Trace.

①  ② ③ ④ ⑤

Look after plants.
Look after them, please!

Lesson 5 Value   **Value:** look after plants   **Language focus:** *Let's water the plants.*

1 Look and say *glass*, *metal*, *paper*, or *plastic*. Which one is different? Circle.

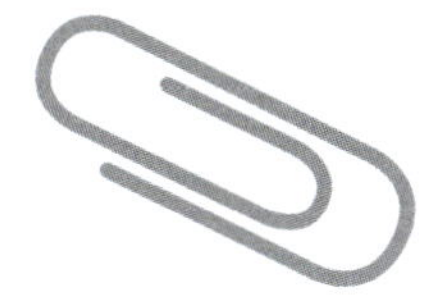   

   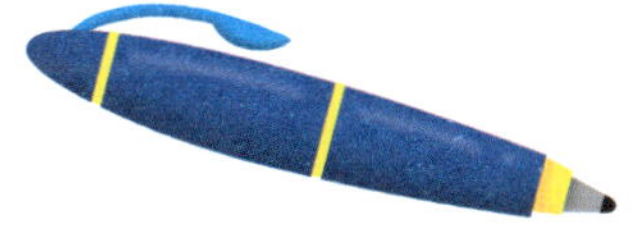

 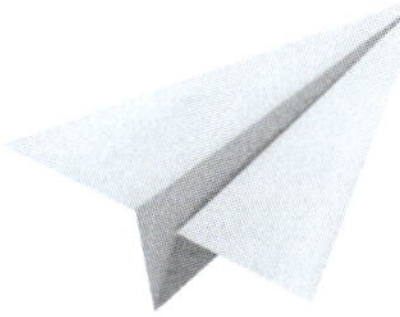  

2 Label the bins: **glass**, **metal**, **paper**, **plastic**.

3 How many things from Activity 1 can you recycle in each bin? Count and write.

Ⓐ 

glass

Ⓑ 

Ⓒ 

Ⓓ 

1 Look and number. **2** 🔊 013 Listen, check, and say. **3** Trace and match.

plant seeds

pick fruit

pull up weeds

dig soil

 Lesson 7 Explore: growing plants　　**Language focus:** *We dig soil / plant seeds / pull up weeds / pick fruit/vegetables.*

1 Look at the pictures. Look at the letters. Write the words.

1  

___ ___ ___ ___ ___

4  

___ ___ ___ ___

2  

___ ___ ___ ___

5  

___ ___ ___ ___ ___ ___

3  

___ ___ ___ ___ ___

6  

___ ___ ___

1 🔊 014 Listen and check ✓.

Ⓐ 

Ⓑ 

2 Draw your plant and color. Trace.

3 Talk about your plant.

My plant needs water and sun.

Lesson 9 Project **Language focus:** *It has two leaves. It needs water and sun.*

1 Circle six words. Write four of the words next to the pictures.

①  ② ③ ④

2 Where are they? Color and say.

| 22 | 23 | 24 | 25 | 26 | 27 |

3 Party time!

1 What can you see? Point and say.

2 🔊015 Look and circle. Listen and check.

I'm six eight .

We're in the town playground . It's a party!

We're at the school river .

We're at the swimming pool park .

3 Check ✓ the celebrations that you go to. Who do you go with?

1 Find five differences. Circle and say.　**2** 🔊 016 Listen and write. Read and check ✓ the correct picture.

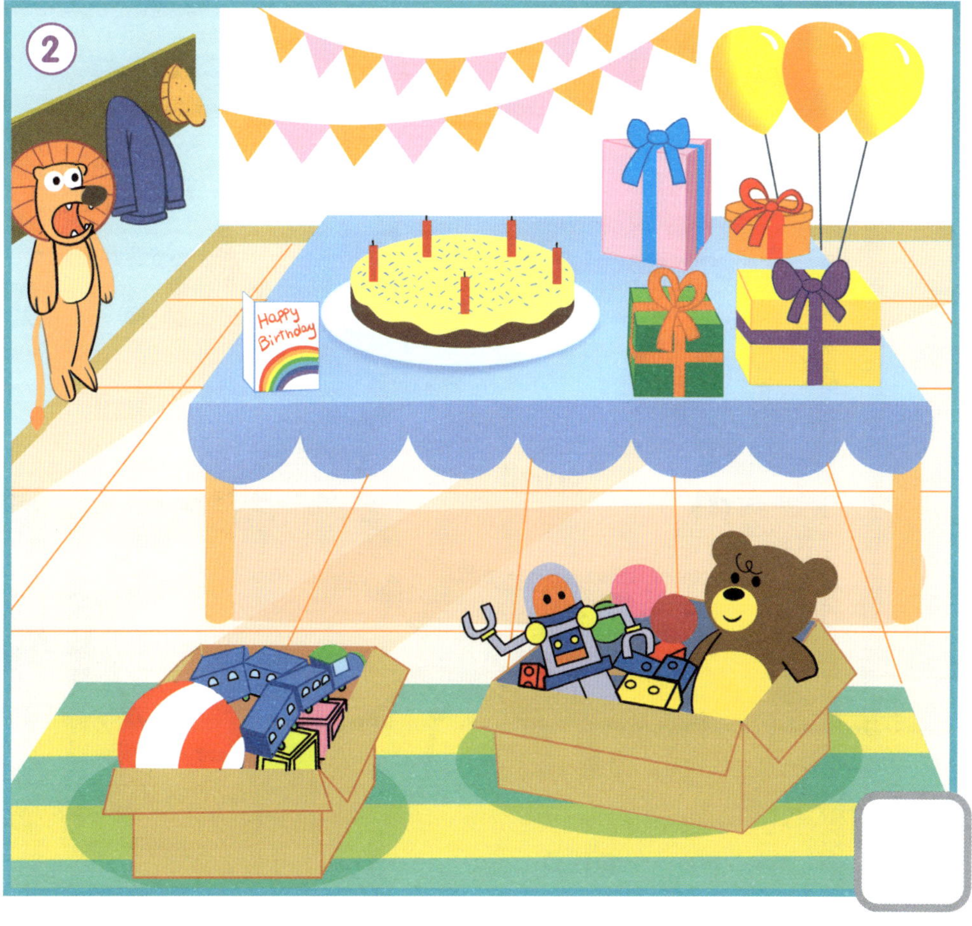

costume ~~cake~~ card presents

1 There are five candles on the ___**cake**___.

2 There are four ___________.

3 There's a ___________. It's a lion.

4 There's a ___________ on the table.
It's a rainbow.

1 Look, say, and follow the /eɪ/ sounds. **2** ◀))017 Listen and check.

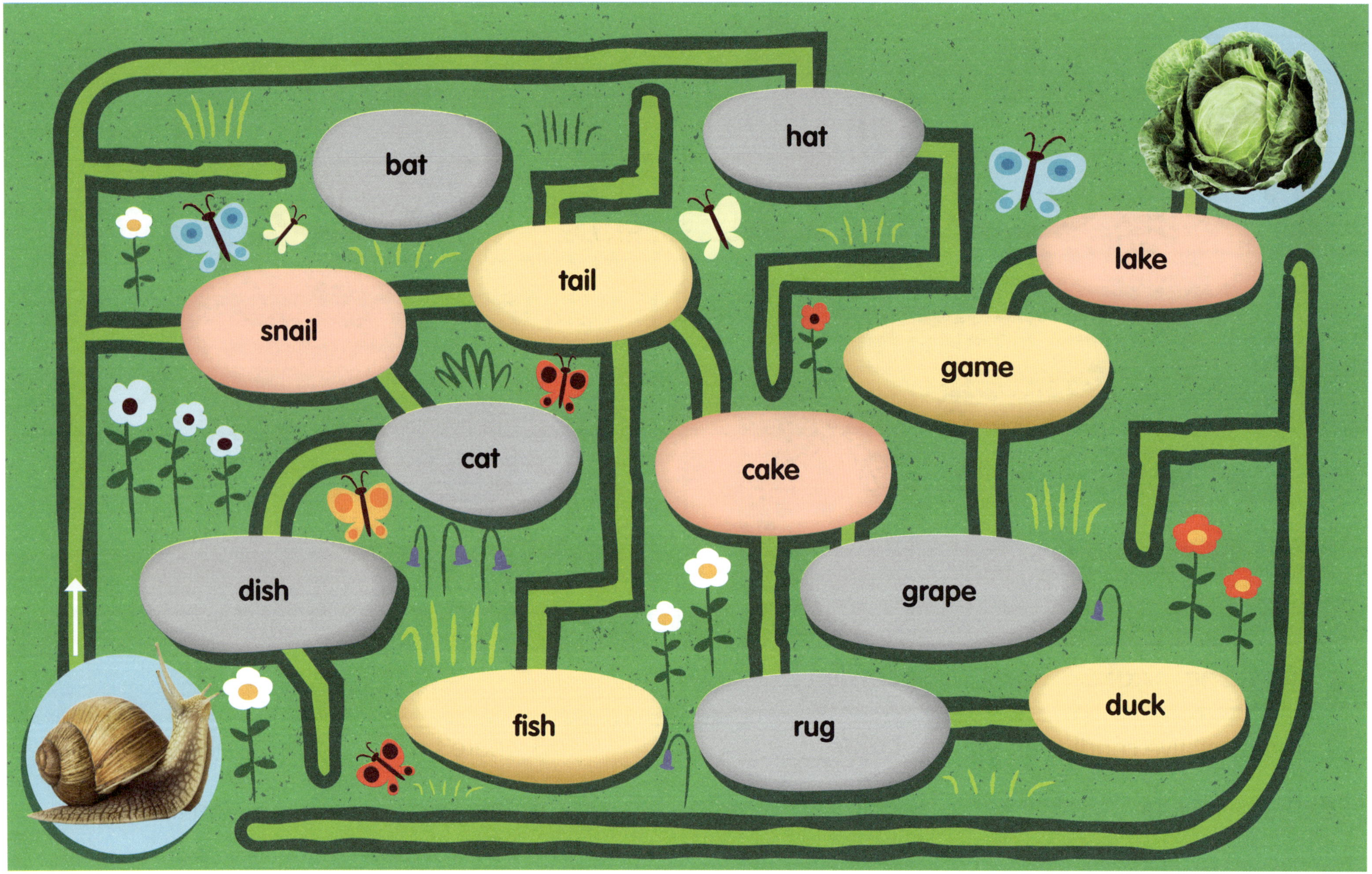

 Lesson 3 Phonics   **Language focus:** /eɪ/ sound with *a_e (lake)* and *ai (snail)*

1  **018** Listen and check ✓ the correct picture.   **2** Where's the party? Circle.

①
Ⓐ
Ⓑ

②
Ⓐ
Ⓑ

③
Ⓐ
Ⓑ

1 Look and match.   **2** Trace.

Lesson 5 Value   **Value:** make things for your friends   **Language focus:** *This is for you.*

1 Complete the months with **er** or **y**. **2** 🔊019 Listen and write.

| Januar __ | Februar __ | March | April | Ma __ | June | Jul __ |

| August | Septemb __ __ | Octob __ __ | Novemb __ __ | Decemb __ __ |

3 When is your birthday? Tell your friend.

3

1 Look and write. music fireworks

2 Find, count, and write.

There are __________ lanterns.

There are __________ bird costumes.

__________________________ candles.

1 Look and read. Write **Yes** or **No**.   **2** Color the picture.

1 There's a festival.   _Yes_

2 Dan's wearing a bird costume.   _No_

3 There are lanterns.   _______

4 There are cakes.   _______

5 It's September.   _______

6 There are decorations.   _______

1 Look and write the color.   yellow   orange   red   blue   green

2 Look at the numbers and color. Use the key.   **3** Count and say *There are … .*

1 🔊 020 Listen and color.   **2** Draw lines. Look at the letters. Write the words.

Our communities | Now I know

1 Match and say.　**2** Find, color, and say.　**3** Circle the children who are helping.

cook　　cleaner　　beach　　cake　　paper　　August

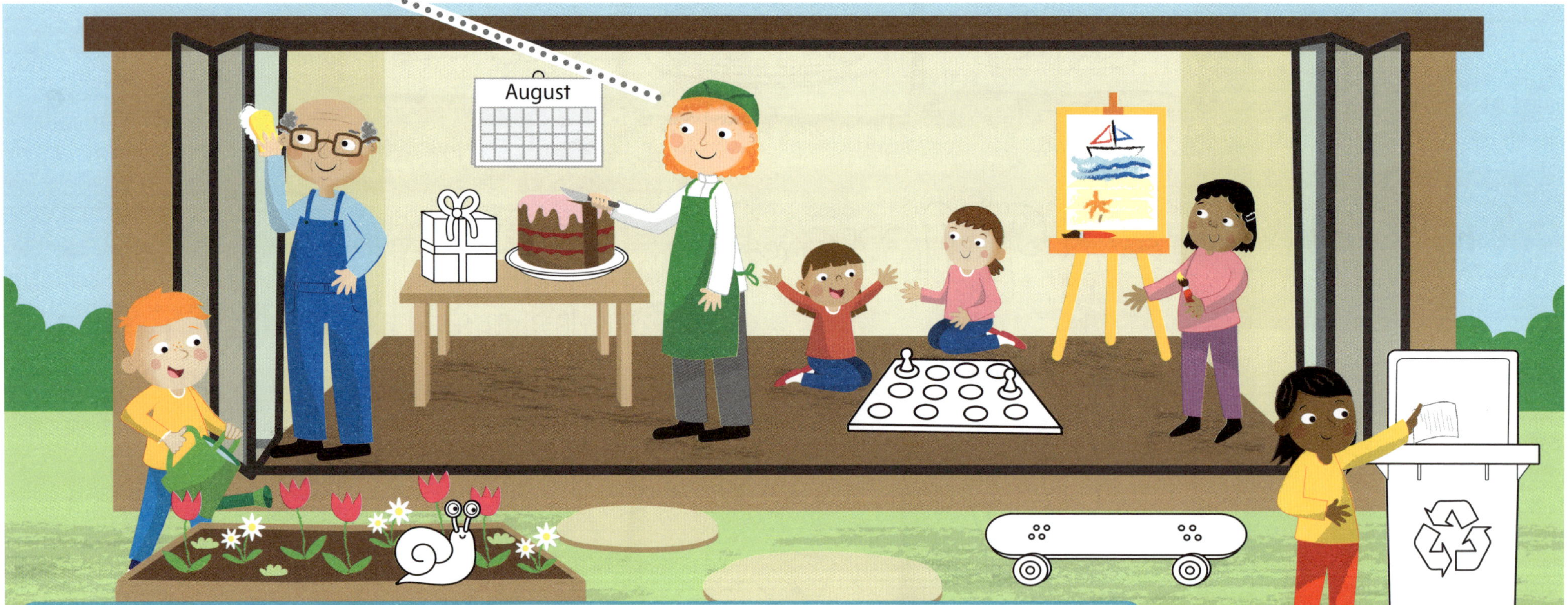

1 Plan a party for your community. Use the words in the boxes or your own ideas.

Who? teacher firefighter friends mom grandpa

Things to do play board games dress up dance watch fireworks

Where? beach yard playground school

Food cake fruit vegetables lemonade

2 Draw your party and say.

My party

Who?

____

Where?

____

Things to do

____

Food

____

1 Who's missing? Match and say.
2 Look and write.

police   grandma   driver   cleaner

bus __________   __________   __________ **officer**   __________

3 What do you think? Write and say.

 okay    good    amazing

I think this story is __________________________.

1 🔊**021** Look, listen, and number.

Nina waters the plants. The zucchini plants are very big!

It's time to pick the zucchinis. There are lots!

The plants grow. Arturo and Nina pull up weeds.

What are these? They're zucchini seeds.

2 What do they eat or drink in the story? Check ✓.

A

B

C

D

E

F

G

H

Let's create!

1 Look and match.   **2** 🔊 022 Listen and number the people.

masks   decorations   stage   books   lantern

1 🔊 023 Listen and check ✓.

Ⓐ

Ⓑ

Ⓒ

2 🔊 024 Listen and write.

4 Things we make

1 Look and match. Write.

2 Circle the materials you use at school.   3 What do you like making? Say.

A

B

C

Lesson 1 Introduction   **Unit 4 focus:** art

1 🔊025 Listen and write. **2** Read, look, and circle.
3 🔊026 Listen and check ✓ the correct picture.

tape   paintbrush   camera

1 027 Listen and check ✓ the words with the /u/ sound.

2 028 Choose the color with the same sound. Color. Listen and check.

blue green

① 

② 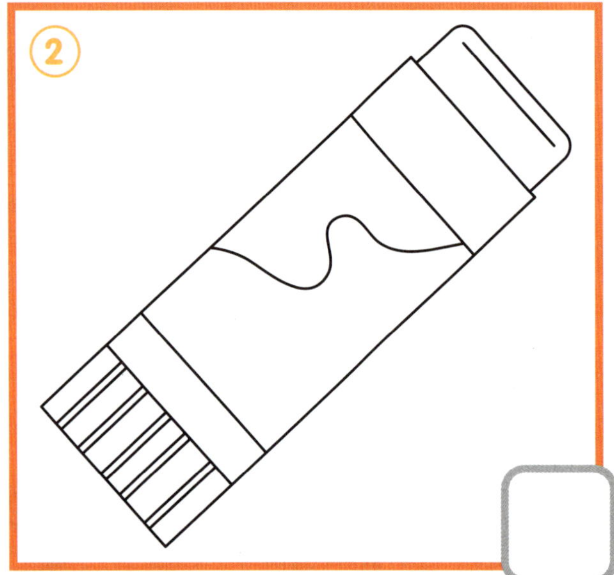

③ 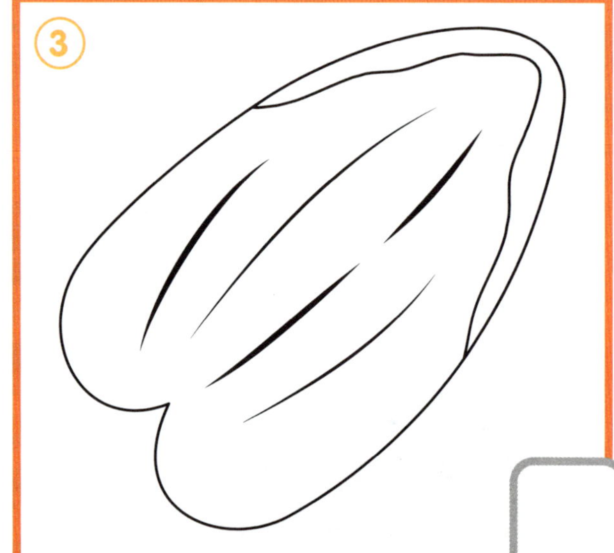

④ 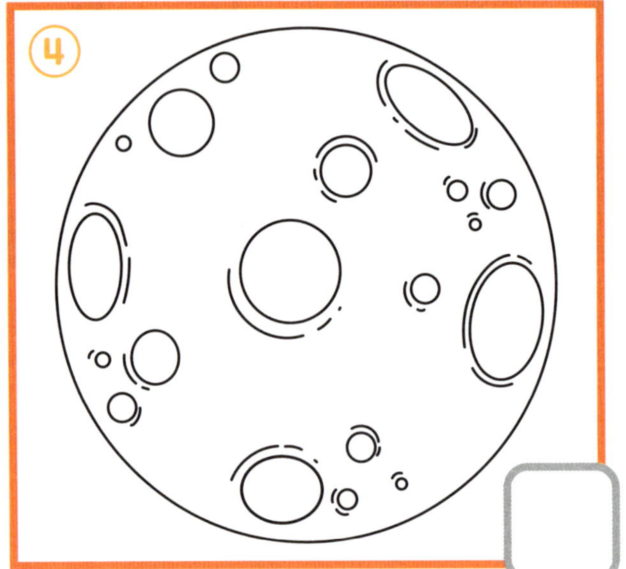

⑤ 

⑥ 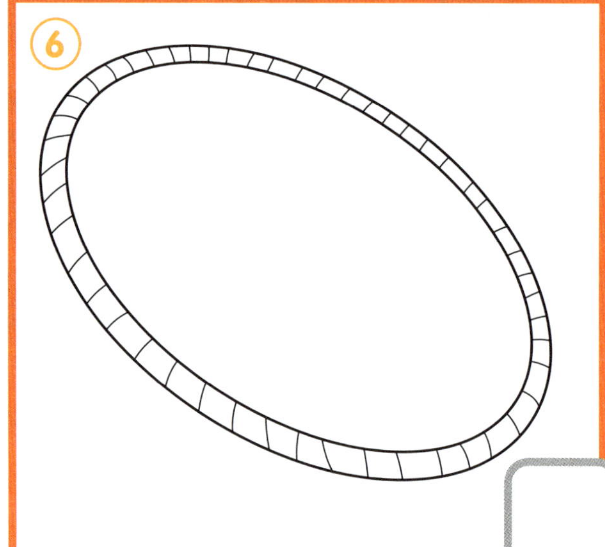

Lesson 3 Phonics   **Language focus:** /u/ sound with *oo (boot)* and *ue (glue)*

1 Read and number. Tell the story.

2 What don't they have? Circle.

4

1 🔊029 Look, listen, and number.

2 🔊030 Listen and complete the song.

is   friend   There

Ask a __________.

Talk it through.

__________ __________ always something you can do.

1 Read and match.

2 What do you like doing? Write.

I like ___________________________.

1 Look and complete.

① 

s__ __ __t line

② 

l__ __g line

③ 

c__ __ __ __d
line

④ 

s__ __ __ __ght line

2 🔊031 Listen and draw.

①   ②   ③   ④

3 Look and copy. How many straight and curved lines are there? Count and say.

① 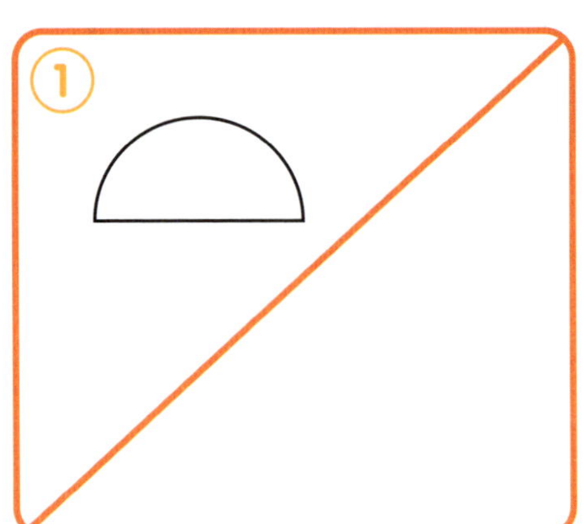

② 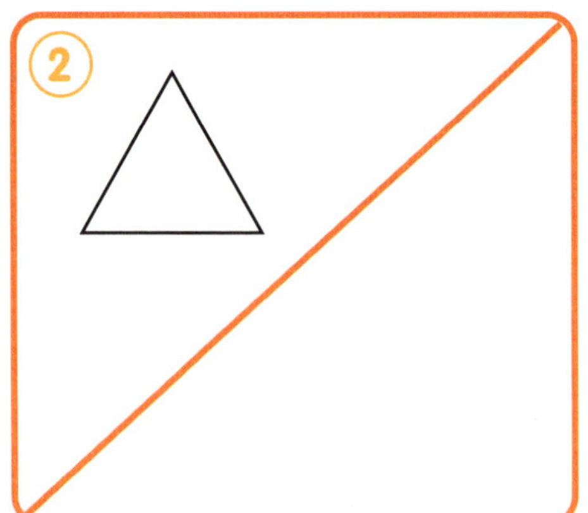

③ 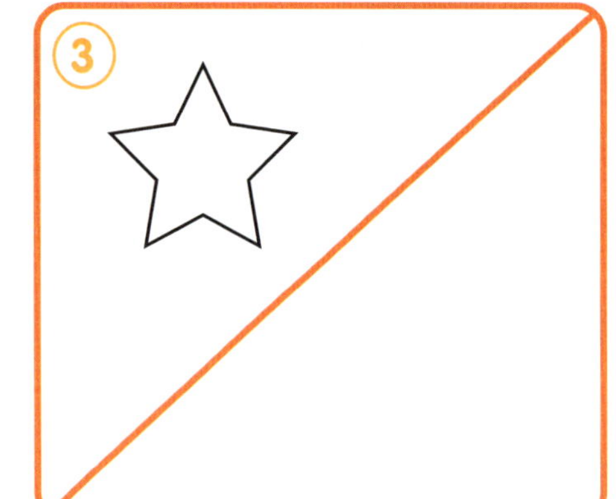

④ 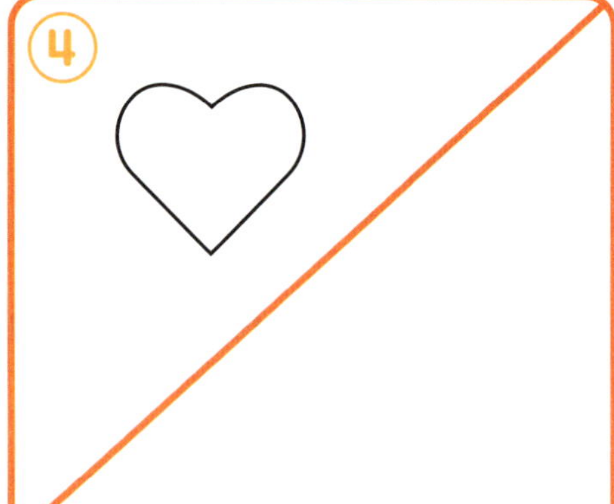

Lesson 7 Explore: lines   **Language focus:** *There are (two) short / long / straight / curved lines.*

1 Look and read. Put a ✓ or an ✗.

These are scissors. ✓

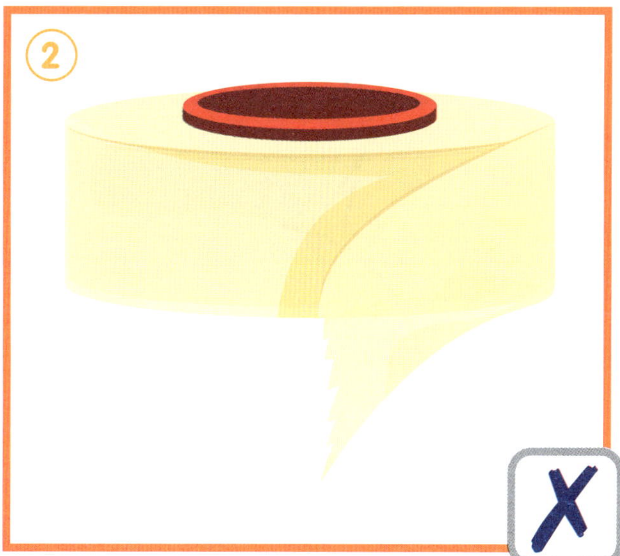

This is clay. ✗

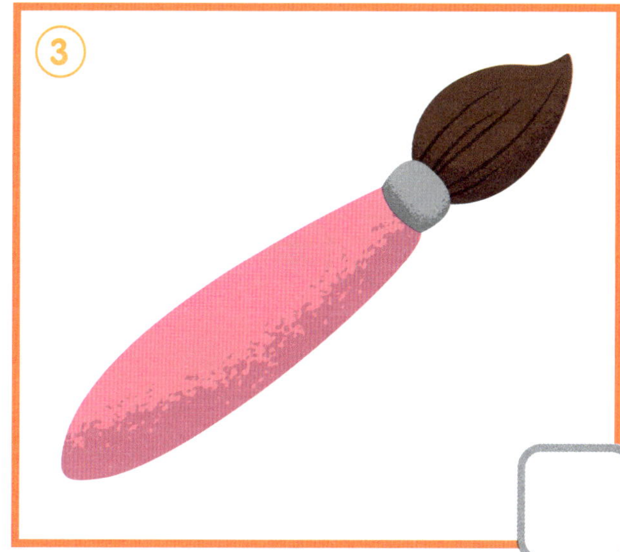

This is a paintbrush.

These are paints.

This is a camera.

These are scissors.

1 Trace and color. Draw your own pattern in the last square.

2 🔊032 Listen and number.

1 Look and write. **printing painting sticking drawing taking making**

2 Find, count, and write.

There are __________ scissors, __________ cameras, and __________ paintbrushes.

5 Stories

1 Where can we find stories? Look and point.
2 🔊033 Listen and number.
3 Draw your favorite storybook. Write the name.

A reading books

B playing with puppets

C skateboarding

D dressing up

E making food

F watching TV

1 🔊 034 Listen, read, and do the maze. Go ←, →, ↑, or ↓. **2** Do the actions in order and say.

Start

laugh

yawn

whisper

whisper

make a face

shout

frown

shout

yawn

whisper

make a face

laugh

frown

laugh

yawn

shout

Finish

5

1 🔊035 Listen, read, and complete. (**night ride**)

I can r __ d __ my bike at n __ __ __ t.

2 🔊036 Listen. Find and circle three words with the /aɪ/ sound.   **3** 🔊037 Listen again and color.

There's a red bike and a pink kite. There's a green light.

   Lesson 3 Phonics   **Language focus:** /aɪ/ sound with *igh (light)* and *i_e (hide)*

1 (038) Look, listen, and match.　　**2** What does Spark have? Circle.  

① I'm a monster!

② Shhh! Please don't shout. Smoke is sleeping.

③ Forty-eight, forty-nine, fifty. Where are you, Spark?

④ I'm tired. Let's go to sleep.

⑤ Oh no! Shhh, Smoke!

1 🔊 039 Are they respecting others? Listen, look, and circle **Yes** or **No**.

Yes   No

Yes   No

Yes   No

Yes   No

2 🔊 040 Listen and complete the song.

(**school   respect**)   Let's ______________ one another.   In our ______________ and in our town.

1 Look and write. **2** 🔊 041 Listen and number.

superhero   child   king   wolf   bear   scarecrow

3 Connect the dots.

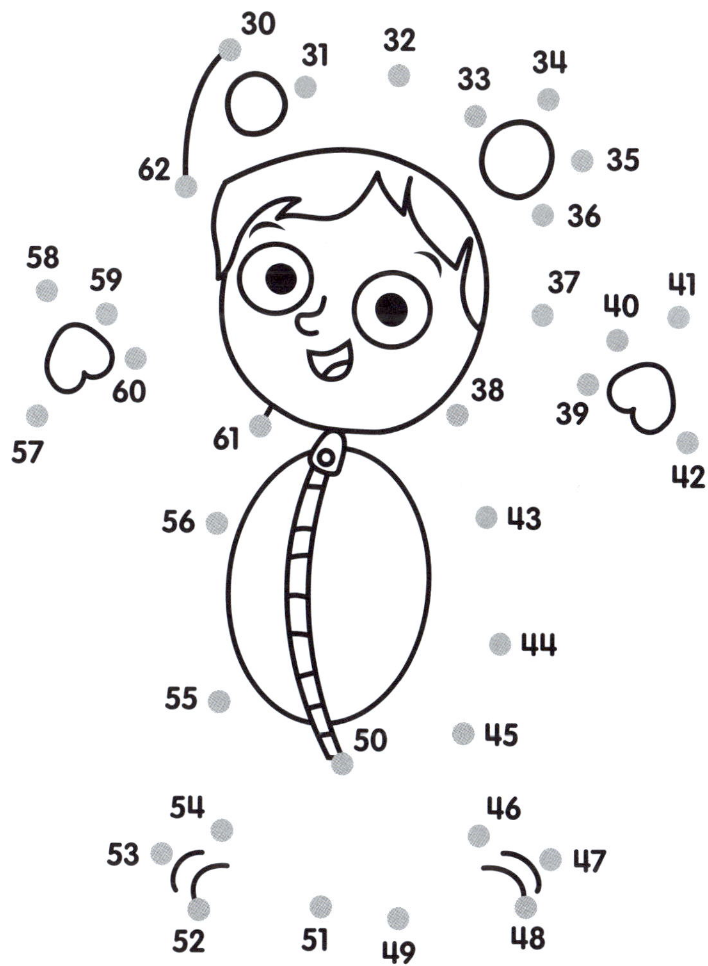

4 Write **Yes, she is**. or **No, she isn't**.

Is she a bear?

____

1 Look and match. **2** Read, circle, and say.

This shadow is a rabbit cow .

This shadow is a bear wolf .

This shadow is a duck goat .

This shadow is a spider bird .

  Lesson 7 Explore: shadows and puppets **Language focus:** *light, dark, shadow, flashlight*

1 🔊 042 Listen and draw lines.

Ben Vee Dan Sam Asma

5

1 🔊 043 Listen and number. **2** Complete.

s d f b k c

__ear

__rog

__uperhero

__ing

__ow

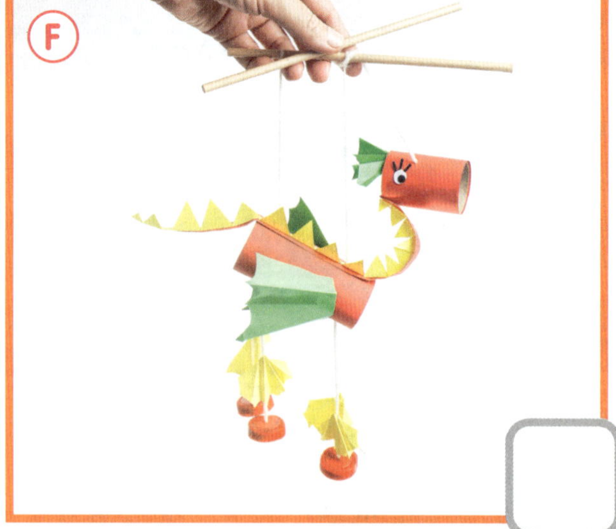

__ragon

Lesson 9 Project   **Language focus:** *Is your puppet a (superhero)? Yes, she/he is. / No, she/he isn't.*

1 Find the words. Look → and ↓ . Write.

whisper

____

____

w	h	i	s	p	e	r
o	a	w	h	o	p	s
l	b	r	a	w	e	y
f	d	h	d	s	f	a
t	f	r	o	w	n	w
r	e	s	w	p	e	n
b	e	a	r	e	i	t

____

____

____

Let's make music!

1 Look and write.   **2** Where do you hear music? Check ✓.   **3**    Listen. Draw 😊 or 😞.

beach   school   home   library   festival   supermarket

1 (045) Listen and check ✓.   **2** Read and write.   **3** Play *Say and point*.

> guitar   tambourine   piano   trumpet   recorder   drum

She's playing the ________________________.

He's banging the ________________________.

She's shaking the ________________________.

He's playing the ________________________.

1 🔊 046 Look, listen, and read. Write.

① 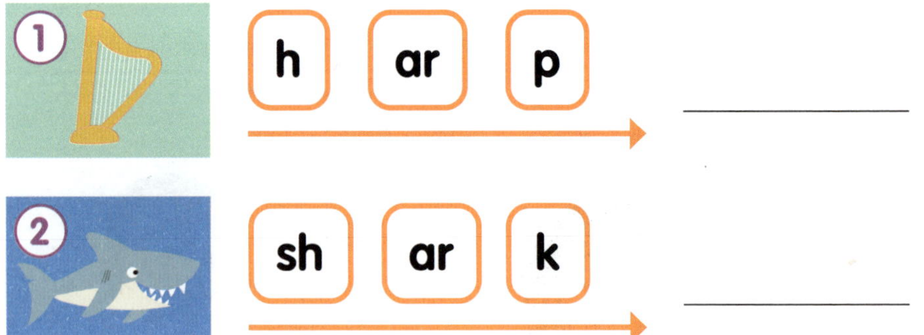 | h | ar | p | → ___________

② | sh | ar | k | → ___________

③ | s | t | ar | → ___________

2 🔊 047 Listen and check ✓ the words with the /ar/ sound.

①  ☐

②  ☐

③  ☐

④  ☐

⑤  ☐

⑥  ☐

Lesson 3 Phonics   **Language focus:** /ar/ sound with *ar* (harp, shark)

1 🔊 048 Read and circle. Listen and check.   **2** Where are they? Circle.

1 Look and match. **2** Point and say *Let's . . . .*

3 049 Listen and complete the song.   (sad   cheer)

I'm __________ today.   Let's __________ you up!

  Lesson 5 Value   **Value:** cheer your friends up   **Language focus:** *I'm sad. Let's cheer you up.*

1 Look and write **Yes** or **No**.   **2** Play the *Opposites* game. Look and do the opposite.

1 The cat is fast. __________

2 The snail is slow. __________

3 The trumpet is quiet. __________

4 The boy is loud. __________

5 The mouse is low. __________

6 The bird is high. __________

1 Look and write. calm cheerful excited scared

2 🔊050 Listen, look, and match.   **3** 🔊051 Listen again and circle your favorite. Say.

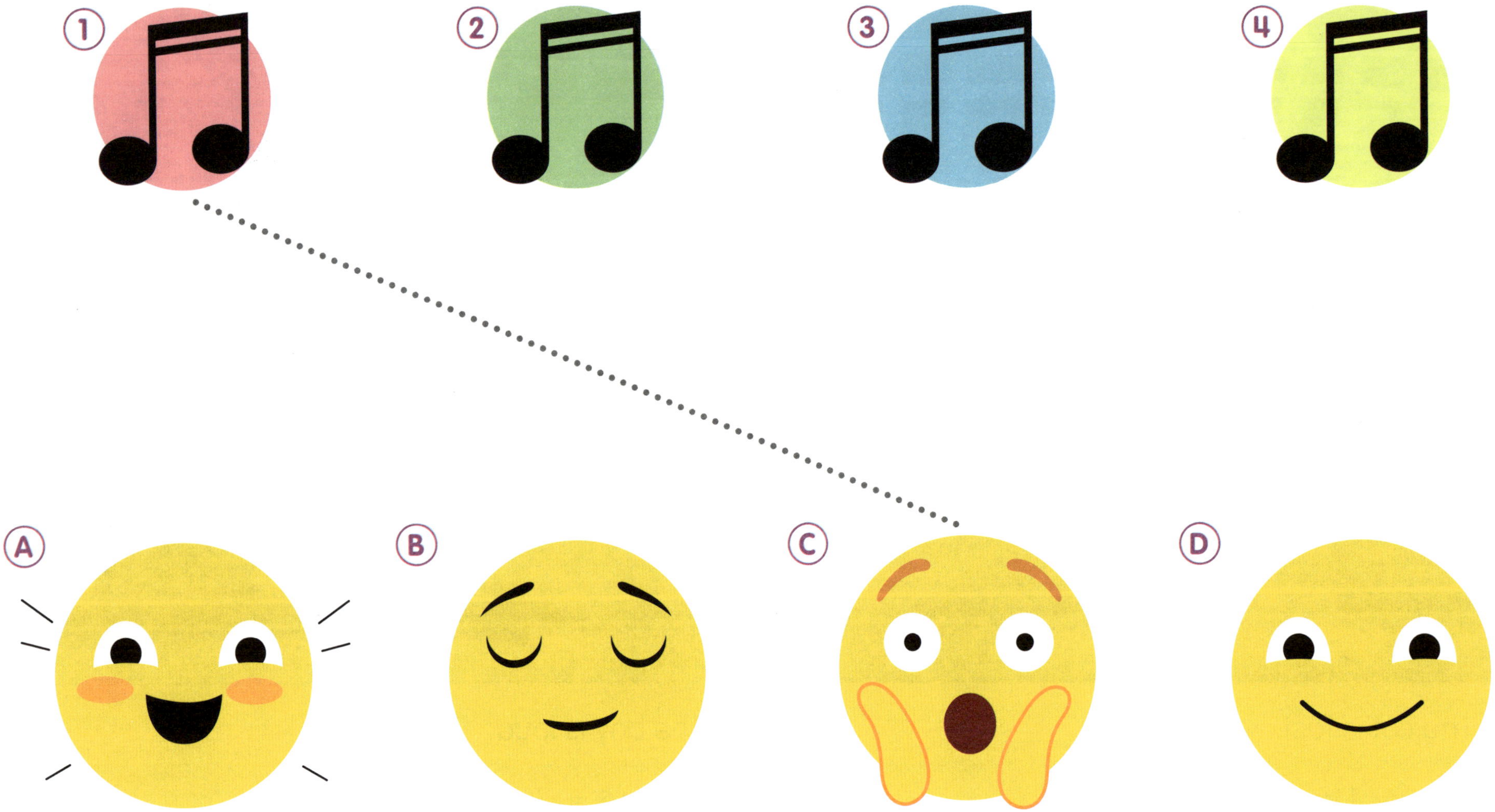

① ② ③ ④

Ⓐ Ⓑ Ⓒ Ⓓ

_______   _______   _______   _______

1 Read this. Choose a word from the box. Write the correct word next to numbers 1–5.

The music festival

There's a music festival in my town today and I'm **1** **excited**. My sister is playing the **2** _______________ and my brother is banging the **3** _______________.

I'm dancing and singing and I'm shaking the **4** _______________. It's loud and fast.

Now I'm eating a **5** _______________. This festival is fun!

excited   tambourine   trumpet   cake   drum

1 Which two pictures are the same? Circle.

2 Choose two pictures. Say what's the same or different. Use the words to help you.

triangles   flowers   bow   shoes   frown   excited   happy
green   pink   yellow   blue   red

3 Look and write the sentence.

banging   She's   drum.   the   _______________________

1 Circle six words. Write four of the words under the pictures.

2 🔊052 Listen and color.

Let's create | Now I know

1 Choose a character. **2** Play the game. Act in character.

bear   king   wolf   scarecrow   superhero

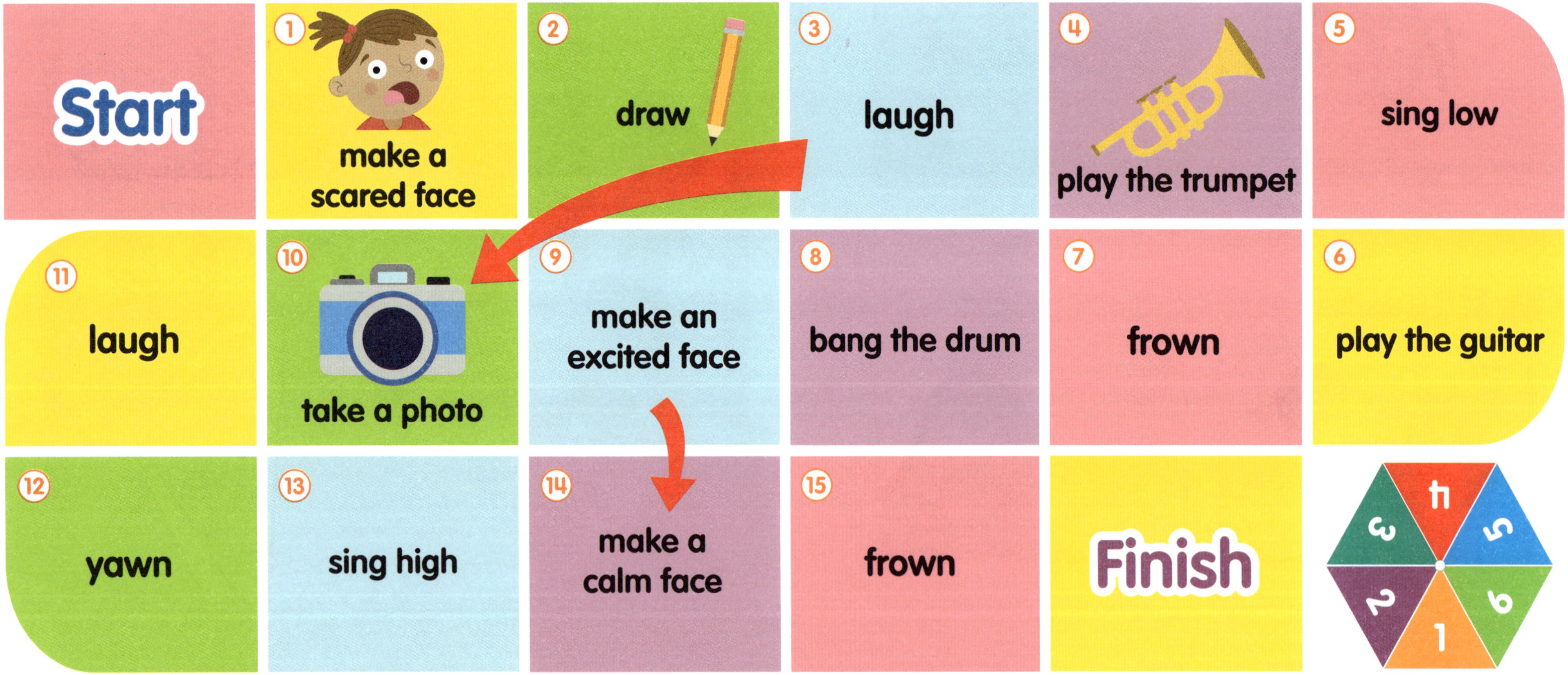

Start	**1** make a scared face	**2** draw	**3** laugh	**4** play the trumpet	**5** sing low
11 laugh	**10** take a photo	**9** make an excited face	**8** bang the drum	**7** frown	**6** play the guitar
12 yawn	**13** sing high	**14** make a calm face	**15** frown	**Finish**	

1 Write sentences about you.

calm   cheerful   excited   scared   sad   tired   angry   happy

Playing a board game makes me feel ____________________.

Painting makes me feel ____________________.

Fireworks make me feel ____________________.

Bears make me feel ____________________.

Shaking the tambourine makes me feel ____________________.

1 🔊 053 Read and connect. Listen and check.

1 Reed loves · · · · · · · · · · · · · · · beautiful song!

2 What a   make music, too!

3 She flies to the village   singing.

4 Birds can   and sits in a tree.

2 Who does Reed meet? Check ✓ and say.

3 What do you think? Write and say.

 okay    good    amazing

I think this story is ___________________________.

Story time What is music?   **Units 4–6 concept:** creativity

1 What's different? Look and say.   **2** Which picture is from the story? Check ✓.

3 🔊054 Listen and write. How does Reed's song make you feel?

sad   calm   excited   cheerful   Reed's song makes me feel ___________________.

On the move

1 Look and match.   **2** Find and circle a bear, a bird, and a bin.

beach   bike   playground   skateboard   guitar

3 Look and write **Yes** or **No**.

1 He's swimming. _________

2 He's frowning. _________

3 She's catching a ball. _________

4 She's wearing a helmet. _________

5 He's wearing red shoes. _________

6 She's running. _________

Lesson 1 Concept   **Units 7–9 concept:** movement   **Language focus:** *land, air, water*

1 055 Listen and check ✓. **2** Write the missing numbers. Say.

A

B

C

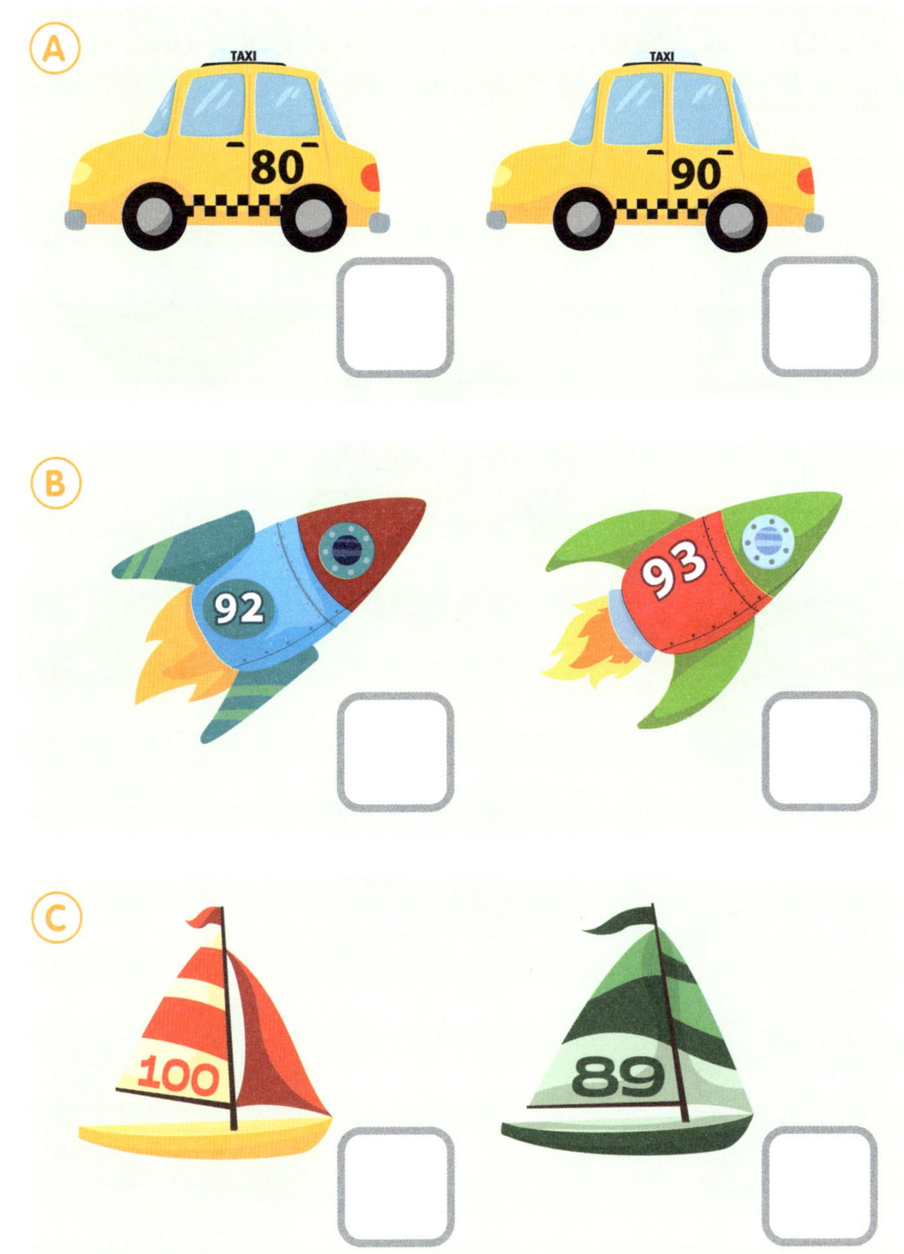

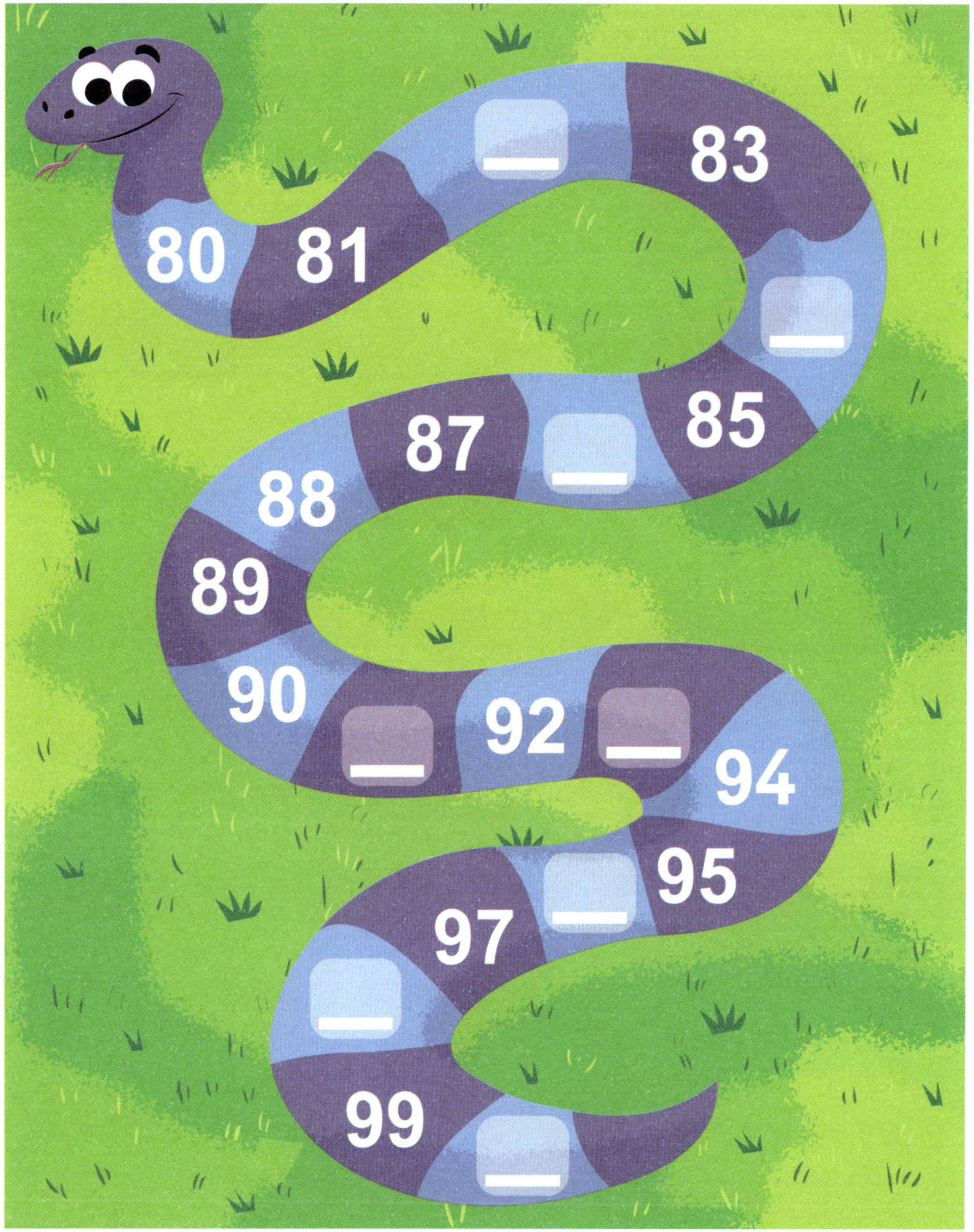

7 Let's go!

1 Look and write. (land   air   water)   **2** Match.   **3** What are they doing? Point and say.

① ____________________

② ____________________

③ ____________________

1 🔊 056 Look and write. Listen and check.   **2** Point and say.

car   bus   walk   train   plane   boat

3 Write.

7

1 🔊 057 Listen and draw the **ar** words and the **er** words.

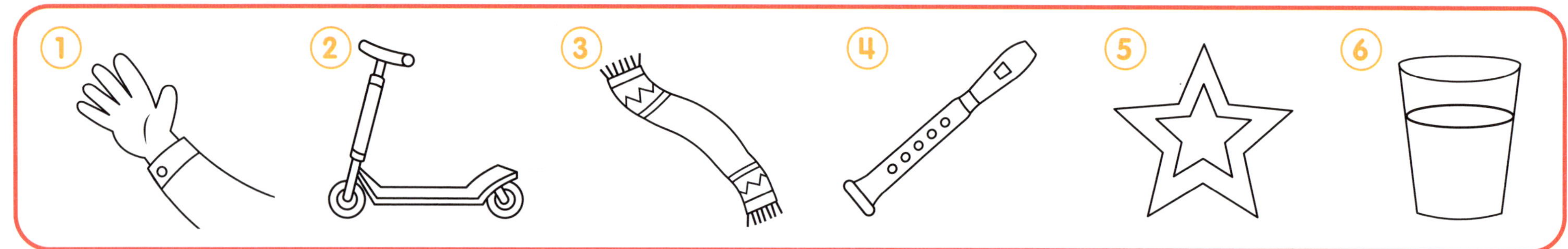

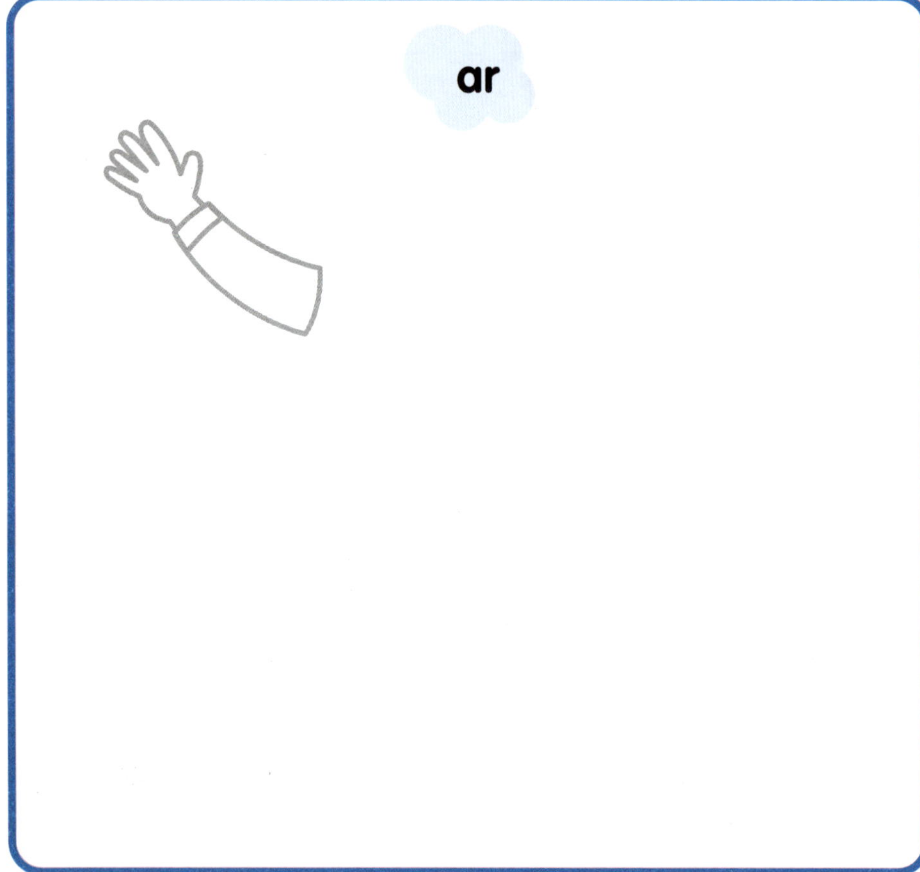

ar

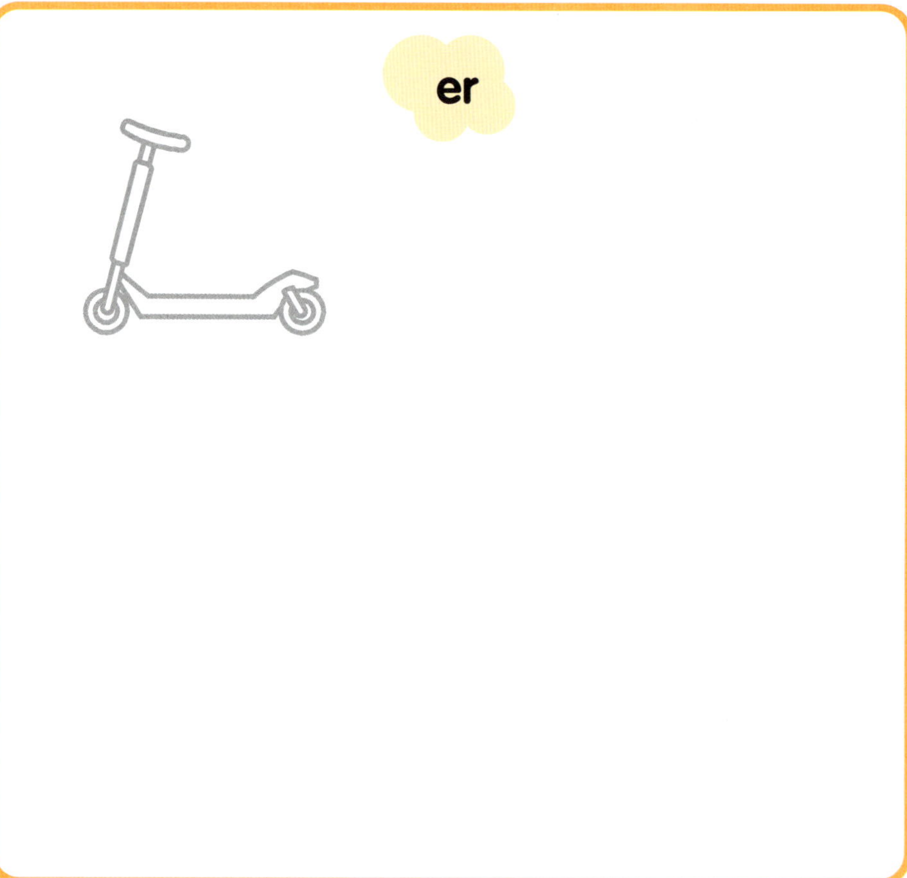

er

Lesson 3 Phonics   **Language focus:** /ər/ sound with *er (scooter, soccer)*

1 Look and number. Tell the story. **2** Who can't fly? Circle.

1 Who is traveling safely? Look and point.

2 🔊058 Listen and complete the song.

road   helmet   bike

Don't run into the ______________.

Wear a ______________ when you ride your ______________.

Lesson 5 Value   **Value:** travel safely   **Language focus:** *We need to wear our helmets.*

1 Look and write.　**2** 🔊059 Listen and draw lines in order.

tractor　flies　drives　truck　motorcycle　taxi

①

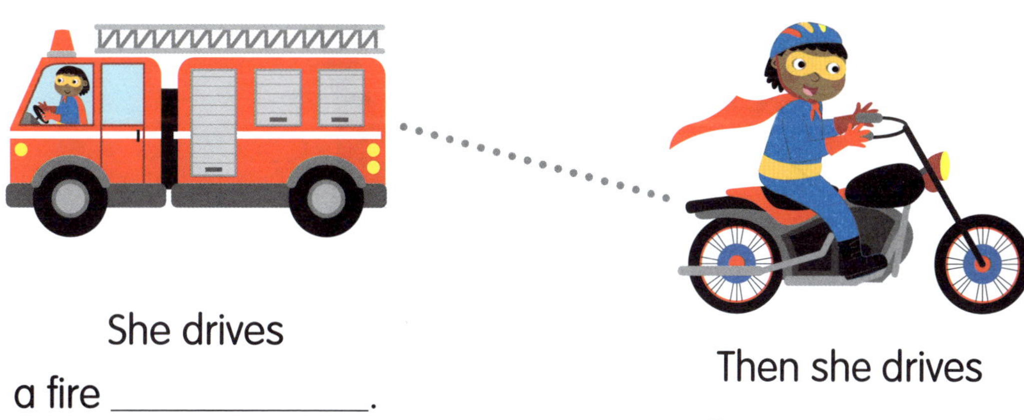

She drives
a fire ______________.

Then she drives
a ______________.

Then she ______________
a helicopter.

②

He ______________ a truck.

Then he drives
a ______________.

Then he drives
a ______________.

1 🔊060 Listen and color. **2** Read and circle.

1 The astronaut is cheerful   sad .

2 The astronaut has a camera   paintbrush .

3 There are 18   19 stars.

4 It's big   small in space.

1 🔊 **061** Read the question. Listen and write a name or a number.

1 What is the girl's name? _____**Cara**_____

2 Is Cara 4 or 5? _________

3 What is the robot's name? _________

4 What is the boy's name? _________

5 Is Dan 6 or 7? _________

1 Read and trace.   **2** Look, draw, and color.

Draw the body .

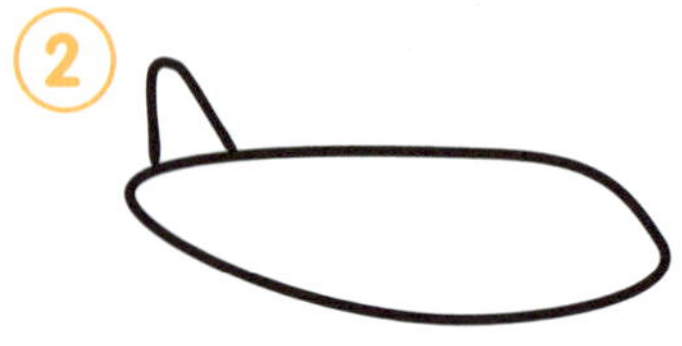

Draw the tail.

Draw the wings.

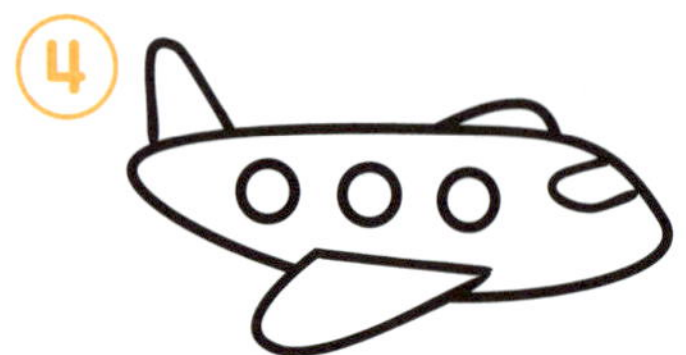

Draw the windows.

Color your plane.

3 Say *My plane is …* . Use the words in the box to help you.

fast   slow   high   low   loud
quiet   red   blue   green   pink
orange   yellow   purple   gray
brown   **black**   big   small

1 Look and write.

scooter   soccer   astronaut
boat   space   taxi   train   ~~bus~~

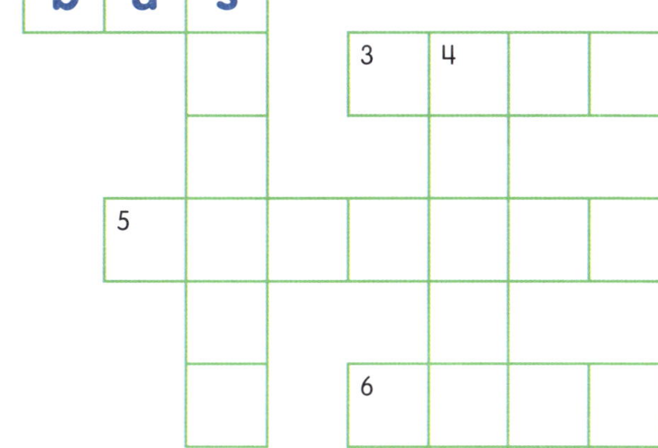

Crossword:
1 b u 2 s
3 4
5
6
7
8

2 Look and write the sentence. Read and check ✓.

hot air balloon.   He   a   flies

____

____

A

B

 Animal action

1 Read and circle. **2** 🔊062 Listen and check.
3 Check ✓ the animals that can jump.

Cats can walk   fly .

Frogs can swim   fly .

Sharks can run   swim .

Cows can walk   dance .

Turtles can fly   swim .

Penguins can fly   swim .

1 Look and complete the questions.   **2** Circle the answers.

(**Do   have**)   (**snakes   rabbits   dolphins   monkeys   tigers**)

① 

Do ______________ have legs?

Yes, they do.   No, they don't.

② 

Do ______________ have wings?

Yes, they do.   No, they don't.

③ 

______ ______________ have tails?

Yes, they do.   No, they don't.

④ 

______ ______________ have tails?

Yes, they do.   No, they don't.

⑤ 

______ ______________ ________ legs?

Yes, they do.   No, they don't.

1 🔊 063 Look, listen, and read. Write.

① 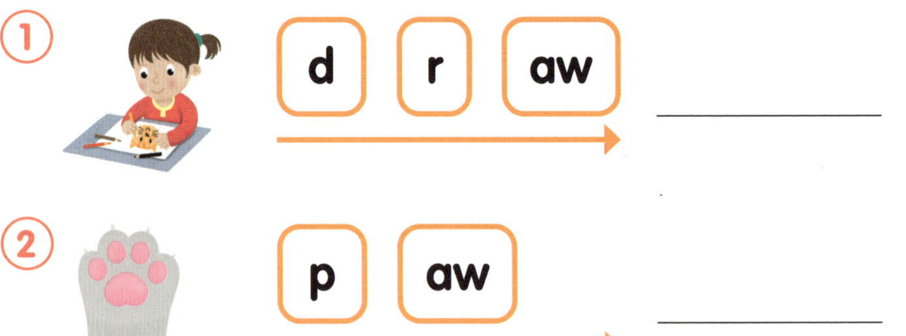 | d | r | aw → __________

② | p | aw → __________

③ | s | ee | s | aw → __________

2 🔊 064 Listen and check ✓ the words with the /ɔ/ sound.

 ①

 ②

 ③

 ④

 ⑤

 ⑥

 Lesson 3 Phonics   **Language focus:** /ɔ/ sound with *aw (paw, claw)*

1 🔊065 Read and circle. Listen and check.   **2** What costumes do they wear? Circle.

1 Write the days.

Thursday   Sunday   Tuesday   Friday

Monday	___________	Wednesday	___________

___________	Saturday	___________

2 Write or draw an activity for each day. Use the words on the page or think of your own activities.

ride a bike

play with a ball

dance

swim

play soccer

1 🔊 066 Listen and number. Write.

snakes   tigers   lizards
rabbits   spiders   monkeys

crawl   leap   hop
climb   swing   slither

A

B

C

D

E

F

1 Take the quiz. Read and answer.

tiger

frog

bear

snake

duck

shark

Which animal is it?

1. This animal swims, walks, and flies. It has webbed feet. __________

2. This animal has webbed feet and strong legs. It jumps high. __________

3. This animal has claws and strong legs. It's orange and black. __________

4. This animal has a smooth body, and it swims. It has big teeth! __________

5. This animal has a smooth body. It slithers. __________

6. This animal has claws and a big body. It can't fly. __________

Lesson 7 Explore: animal adaptations **Language focus:** *webbed feet, strong legs, long tail, smooth body*

1 🔊067 Listen and color.

1 Count, write, and say.   **2** Color the snakes.   **3** Draw and color your snake. Write.

This snake has **12** shapes.

This snake has _________ stripes.

This snake has _________ shapes.

This snake has _________ stripes.

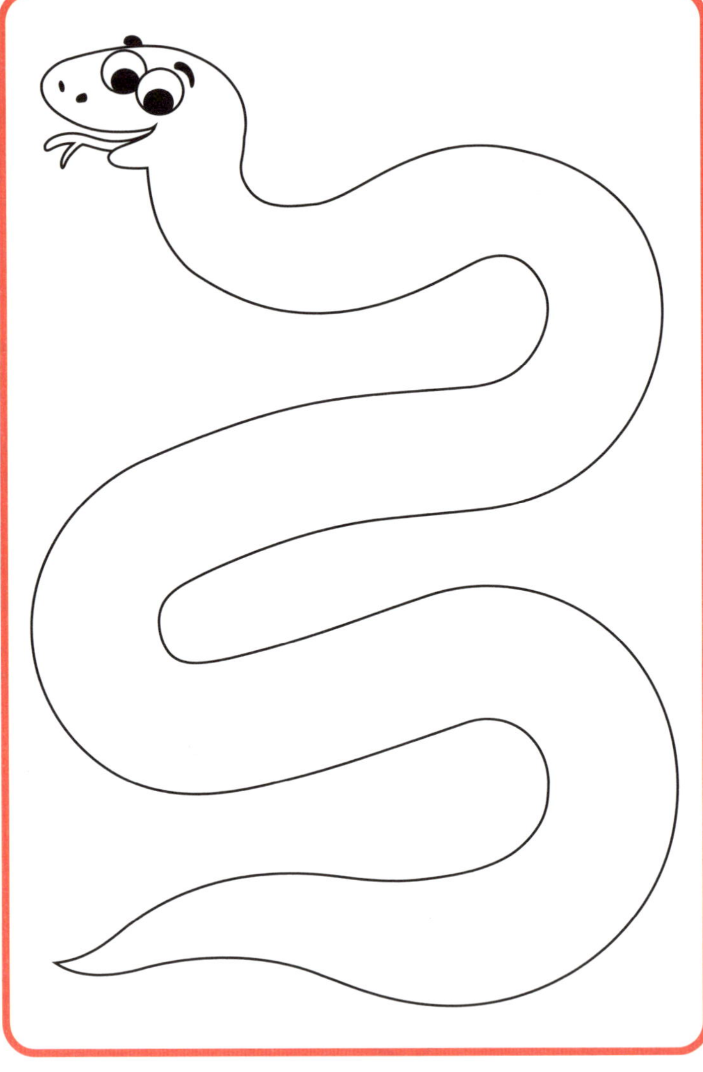

1 Find seven movement words. Look ➡ and ⬇.　**2** Choose a movement word and write.

3 Which animals have strong legs? Point and say.

Rabbits ___________.

Dolphins ___________.

s	l	i	t	h	e	r
w	a	s	s	o	c	e
i	i	f	w	p	o	p
n	c	l	i	m	b	l
g	t	b	m	j	l	e
h	g	m	n	r	k	a
c	r	a	w	l	d	p

Snakes ___________.

Snails ___________.

Tigers ___________.

Monkeys ___________.

Lizards ___________.

Adventures

1. How are they moving? Look and write.
2. Who is slithering? Find and circle.
3. Choose a safe way to move and say *I'm* … .

swinging   running   crawling
jumping   walking   climbing

Lesson 1 Introduction   **Unit 9 focus:** movement and places

1 🔊 **068** Listen and color.   **2** Read and match.   **3** Write.

mountains ocean farm
forest desert city

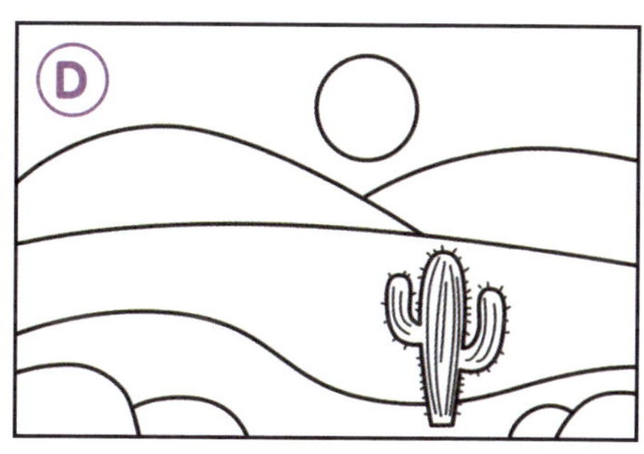

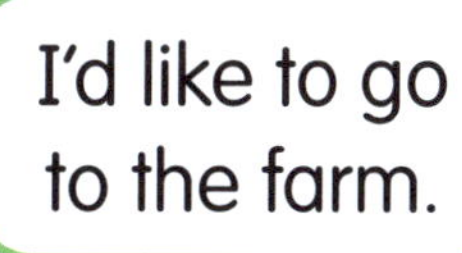

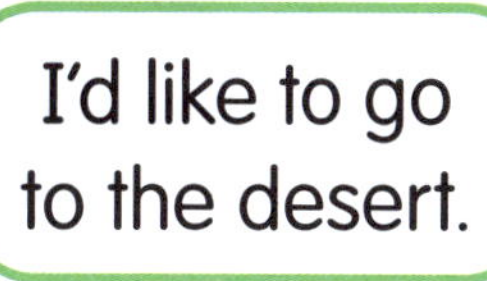

1 🔊069 **Look and listen. Check ✓ the words with the /aʊ/ sound.**

2 🔊070 **Listen again. What is the sound in the other words?**

1 What's missing? Match and say.   **2** Look and write.   **3** Who is cold? Circle.  

a flashlight   a river   two hats   the mountain

  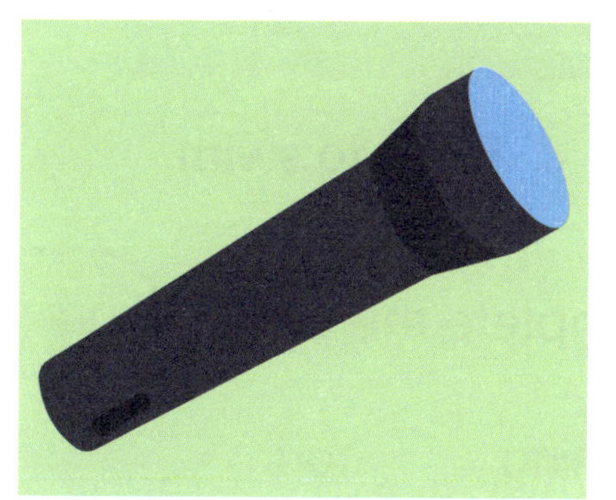 

1 What would you like to try? Check ✓.　　**2** Ask and answer *Would you like to … ?*

climb a mountain

ride a bike

play the piano

learn to swim

draw a lizard

3 🔊071 Listen and complete the song.　　(**yes　grow　try　can**)

You can __________ anything,　　You __________ give it a go.

Say __________ to a challenge　　And that's how you __________.

Lesson 5 Value　　**Value:** accept challenges　　**Language focus:** *Would you like to (climb a mountain)? Yes, I would.*

1 Look and write.
2 🔊072 Listen and check ✓.

skiing   surfing   skating   sailing

1

____

2

zip-lining   _________________________

3

riding a horse   _________________________

3 Draw and write.

Is __________ sailing? _________________________

1 Look and match.

spring

summer

fall

winter

2 Look and write **rainy** or **dry**.   **3** 🔊073 Listen and draw.

① ___________ season

② ___________ season

   Lesson 7 Explore: seasons   **Language focus:** *spring, summer, fall, winter, rainy, dry*

1 Look at the pictures and read the questions. Write one-word answers.

two   no   ~~forest~~   peach   yes   summer   recorder

1 Where are they?   in the __forest__

2 How many people are there?   ______________

3 Is the woman riding a horse?   ______________

4 Is he happy?   ______________

5 What season is it?   ______________

6 What's the woman eating?   a ______________

7 What's the boy doing?   He's playing the

______________.

1 (♪074) Listen and number. **2** Write.

3 What season is it? Point and say *It's spring, summer, fall, winter.*

> mountains   city
> farm   ocean

A

B

C

D

1 Write.

2 Which word is hiding in the yellow squares?

town   forest   ocean   surfing   skating   desert

1 This is a
town .

2 This is a
____________ .

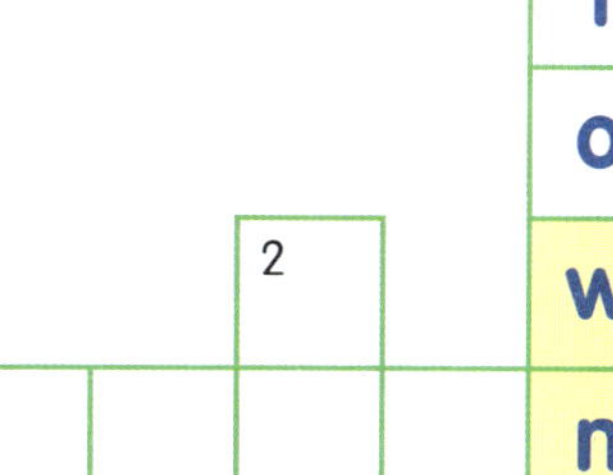

3 This is an
____________ .

4 He's
____________ .

The mystery word is
w __ __ __ __ __ .

5 This is a
____________ .

6 She's
____________ .

3 Look and write the sentence.

go to   the farm.   I'd like to

____

____

4 Where would you like to go?
Draw and write a sentence.

____

____

1 Read the postcards and write.   2 🔊 075 Listen and check.

(calm   swing   lizards   ~~forest~~)

Hello Lara,

I'm in the __forest__. It's sunny and quiet.
There are __________ and monkeys!
The monkeys __________ in the trees.
I feel __________ in the forest.

Bye!

Dan

(taxis   excited   scooter   city   helmet)

Hello Dan,

I'm in the __________. It's big and loud. There are
buses and __________. I ride my __________ to
the park! I need to wear my __________.

I feel __________ in the city.

Bye!

Lara

1 Add your ideas.   **2** Choose and circle words for your postcard.

Places   at the beach   at the farm   in the mountains   in the desert _____________

Adjectives   hot   loud   big _____________

Animals   rabbit   snake   tiger   dolphin _____________

Transportation   boat   plane   train   rocket _____________

Feelings   excited   calm   scared _____________

Actions   leap   hop   swing   climb _____________

3 Write your postcard and draw a picture.

Hello _____________,

I'm _____________. It's _____________.

There are _____________.

I feel _____________.

Bye!

____

1 Read and circle. **2** 🔊076 Listen and check.

1 Ollie lives with his big rabbit mouse family.

2 There are cows and chickens on the farm beach .

3 Ollie wants to see the ocean desert .

4 "The ocean is beautiful cheerful ," thinks Ollie.

5 Ollie sees a big blue white bird at the ocean.

3 Write.

1 Ollie smells the _____air_____.

2 Ollie feels the _____________.

3 Ollie hears the _____________.

4 Ollie tastes the _____________.

4 What do you think? Write and say.

okay

good

😊 **amazing**

I think this story is _____________________.

1 Look and write.   **2** Follow the maze to take Ollie to the ocean.

3 Find and circle the four hiding animals. Say *There's a … .*   **4** 🔊 **077** Listen, point, and say *It's the … .*

forest   mountains   ocean   farm

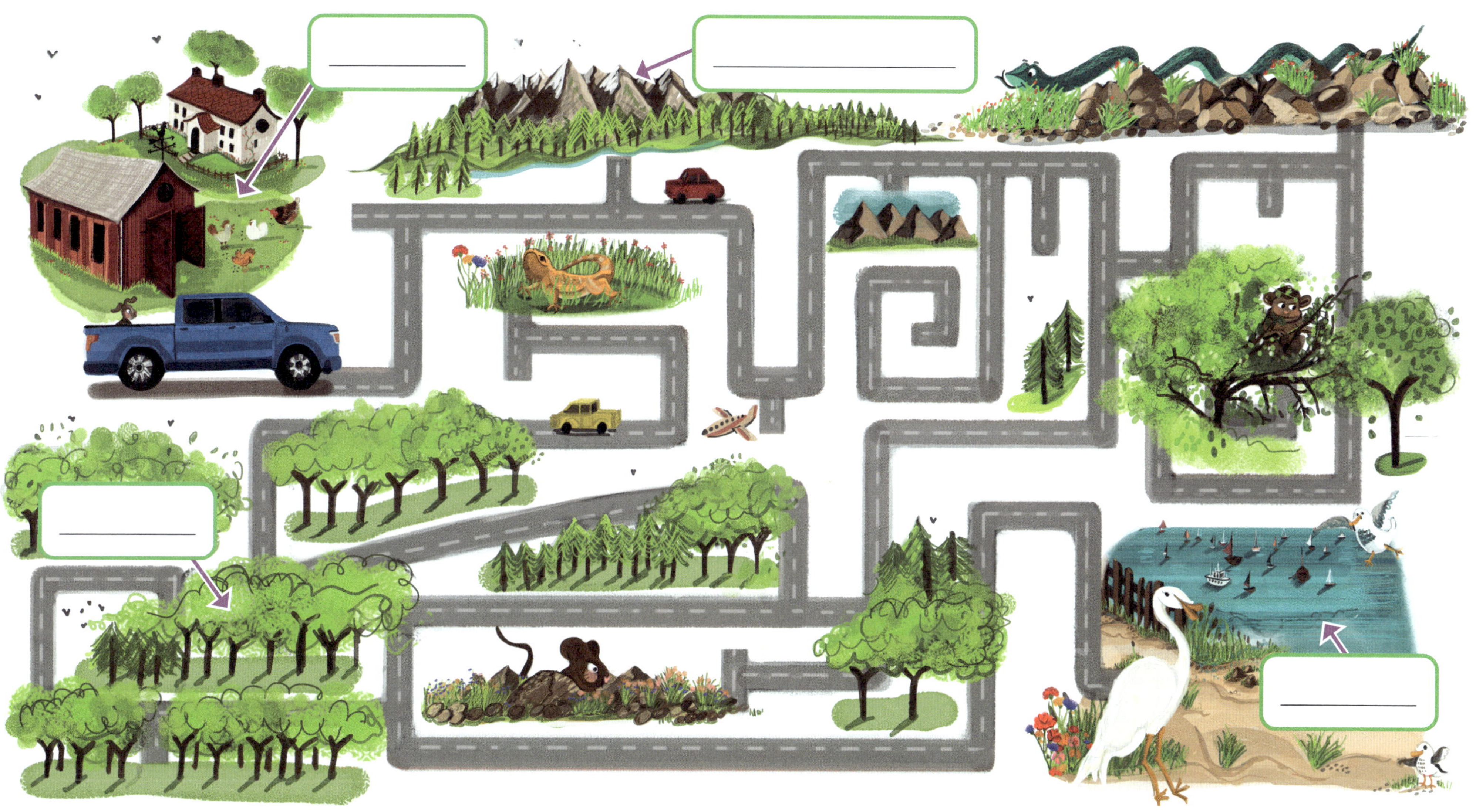

OXFORD
UNIVERSITY PRESS

Great Clarendon Street, Oxford, OX2 6DP, United Kingdom

Oxford University Press is a department of the University of Oxford.
It furthers the University's objective of excellence in research, scholarship,
and education by publishing worldwide. Oxford is a registered trade
mark of Oxford University Press in the UK and in certain other countries

ISBN: 978 0 19 486310 0   Little Blue Dot Activity Book 3

Printed and bound in Portugal by Gráfica Maiadouro

This book is printed on paper from certified and well-managed sources

ACKNOWLEDGEMENTS

Illustrations by: Alejandra Barajas/Advocate Art pp. 38, 39; Claudio Cerri/
Beehive pp. 7, 13, 17, 27, 33, 43, 63, 79, 106, 108; Helen Graper/Beehive pp. 5,
11, 14, 21, 31, 34, 42, 47, 56, 61, 66, 73, 78, 85, 90, 99, 102, 104, 107; Sarah
Lawrence pp. 10, 22, 30, 36, 46, 51, 62, 72, 83, 92, 103; Ed Myer pp. 8, 12, 23,
25, 35, 41, 44, 49, 57, 70, 77, 80, 96; Kevin Payne/Advocate Art pp. 9, 19, 29,
45, 55, 64, 65, 68, 81, 84, 91, 101; Mark Ruffle pp. 18, 20, 28, 50, 54, 58, 71,
86, 94, 95; Angelika Scudamore/Advocate Art pp. 4, 15, 24, 26, 32, 40, 52, 59,
67, 71, 76, 82, 89, 93, 98, 105; Naomi Skinner/The Bright Agency pp. 110, 111;
Ola Szpunar/The Bright Agency pp. 74, 75.

*The publisher would like to thank the following for permission to reproduce
photographs*: 123RF (photochicken); Getty Images (Indeed/ABSODELS,
AlbertPego/Liudmila Chernteska/Julianwphoto/iStock, Ferrantraite/E+,
Matteo Colombo/Ariel Skelley/DigitalVision, Ed Reschke/Martin Ruegner/
Stone, SelectStock/Vetta, Silke Woweries/Herbert Kehrer/The Image Bank,
Jose Luis Pelaez Inc/DigitalVision, Granger Wootz/Tetra Images, Ernst
Glas/500px, Elena Zaretskaya/David Merron Photography/Vicki Jauron,
Babylon and Beyond Photography/Chase Dekker Wold-Life Images/
Alexander Spatari/Moment); Shutterstock (StockLite, fizkes, Sylv1rob1,
Ljupco Smokovski, Khorzhevska, Khannanova Margarita, Susan Law
Cain, Vladimir Nenezic, FrimuFilms Aleksandar Dickov, Palokha Tetiana,
Baryshnikova Irina, worradirek, Luis Molinero, Prostock-studio, Anatoliy
Karlyuk, Martin Good, Napat Aor70, Anne Coatesy, Yuganov Konstantin,
Chani Friedman, Elena Chevalier, Karkas, Natalia K, soo hee kim, LeonP,
Theeradech Sanin, Irin-k, Sharomka, Pavel Savchuk, Mega Pixel, Ronald
Sumners, Elena Scweitzer, PixMarket, Fotokostic, Vacclav, Aaron Alien,
sripfoto, Dinesh Hukmani, Barat Roland, Jacob Lund, Salparadis, Andrei
Armiagov, Eric Buermeyer, Neophuket, Fotogrpahix.ch, Magdanatka, 9nong,
Yevhenii Chulovskyi, Wang LiQiang, Huy Thoai, Seitumer Curlu, Mufti Adi
Utomo, Dionisvera, Bildagentur Zoonar GmbH, Lithium366, Anatoliy Karlyuk,
Taiga, apstockphoto, ventdusud, Evgeniy pavloski Andrew Angelov).

Cover: Getty; kali9, Shutterstock; artjazz, Avesun, cz, Kitsana1980, piyaphon,
Vandathai, evaurban, Kuttelvaserova Stuchelova, Lilkin, Mark Brandon, Marti
Bug Catcher, Martina Fornal, Mark Brandon, pio3, Sergey Novikov.